Cover Design by OfficeLife Essentials

Paperback

This book belongs to:

Date:_____

Notes:

_____
_____
_____
_____
_____
_____
_____
_____
_____
_____
_____
_____
_____

Could this have been an email? ☐ Yes ☐ No

Date:_____

Notes:

_____

_____

_____

_____

_____

_____

_____

_____

_____

_____

_____

_____

_____

Could this have been an email? ☐ Yes ☐ No

Date:_____

Notes:

_____

_____

_____

_____

_____

_____

_____

_____

_____

_____

_____

_____

_____

_____

_____

_____

Could this have been an email? ☐ Yes ☐ No

Date:_____

Notes:

_____

_____

_____

_____

_____

_____

_____

_____

_____

_____

_____

_____

_____

Could this have been an email? ☐ Yes ☐ No

Date:_____

Notes:

_____

_____

_____

_____

_____

_____

_____

_____

_____

_____

_____

_____

_____

Could this have been an email? ☐ Yes ☐ No

Date:_____

Notes:

_____

_____

_____

_____

_____

_____

_____

_____

_____

_____

_____

_____

Could this have been an email? ☐ Yes ☐ No

Date:_____

Notes:

_____

_____

_____

_____

_____

_____

_____

_____

_____

_____

_____

_____

_____

_____

Could this have been an email? ☐ Yes ☐ No

Date:_____

Notes:

_____

_____

_____

_____

_____

_____

_____

_____

_____

_____

_____

_____

_____

Could this have been an email? ☐ Yes ☐ No

Date:_____

Notes:

_____

_____

_____

_____

_____

_____

_____

_____

_____

_____

_____

_____

_____

_____

Could this have been an email? ☐ Yes ☐ No

Date:_____

Notes:

_____

_____

_____

_____

_____

_____

_____

_____

_____

_____

_____

_____

Could this have been an email? ☐ Yes ☐ No

Date:_____

Notes:

_____

_____

_____

_____

_____

_____

_____

_____

_____

_____

_____

_____

_____

_____

_____

Could this have been an email? ☐ Yes ☐ No

Date:_____

Notes:

_____

_____

_____

_____

_____

_____

_____

_____

_____

_____

_____

_____

_____

Could this have been an email? ☐ Yes ☐ No

Date:_____

Notes:

_____

_____

_____

_____

_____

_____

_____

_____

_____

_____

_____

_____

_____

Could this have been an email? ☐ Yes ☐ No

Date:_____

Notes:

_____

_____

_____

_____

_____

_____

_____

_____

_____

_____

_____

Could this have been an email? ☐ Yes ☐ No

Date:_____

Notes:

_____

_____

_____

_____

_____

_____

_____

_____

_____

_____

_____

_____

_____

_____

_____

Could this have been an email? ☐ Yes ☐ No

Date:_____

Notes:

_____

_____

_____

_____

_____

_____

_____

_____

_____

_____

_____

_____

Could this have been an email? ☐ Yes ☐ No

Date:_____

Notes:

_____

_____

_____

_____

_____

_____

_____

_____

_____

_____

_____

_____

_____

_____

Could this have been an email? ☐ Yes ☐ No

Date:_____

Notes:

_____

_____

_____

_____

_____

_____

_____

_____

_____

_____

_____

_____

Could this have been an email? ☐ Yes ☐ No

Date:_____

Notes:

_____
_____
_____
_____
_____
_____
_____
_____
_____
_____
_____
_____
_____
_____

Could this have been an email? ☐ Yes ☐ No

Date:_____

Notes:

_____

_____

_____

_____

_____

_____

_____

_____

_____

_____

_____

_____

Could this have been an email? ☐ Yes ☐ No

Date:_____

Notes:

_____

_____

_____

_____

_____

_____

_____

_____

_____

_____

_____

_____

_____

Could this have been an email? ☐ Yes ☐ No

Date:_____

Notes:

_____

_____

_____

_____

_____

_____

_____

_____

_____

_____

_____

_____

_____

Could this have been an email? ☐ Yes ☐ No

Date:_____

Notes:

_____

_____

_____

_____

_____

_____

_____

_____

_____

_____

_____

_____

_____

_____

_____

Could this have been an email? ☐ Yes ☐ No

Date:_____

Notes:

_____

_____

_____

_____

_____

_____

_____

_____

_____

_____

_____

_____

Could this have been an email? ☐ Yes ☐ No

Date:_____

Notes:

_____

_____

_____

_____

_____

_____

_____

_____

_____

_____

_____

_____

_____

_____

Could this have been an email? ☐ Yes ☐ No

Date:_____

Notes:

_____

_____

_____

_____

_____

_____

_____

_____

_____

_____

_____

_____

Could this have been an email? ☐ Yes ☐ No

Date:_____

Notes:

_____

_____

_____

_____

_____

_____

_____

_____

_____

_____

_____

_____

_____

_____

_____

Could this have been an email? ☐ Yes ☐ No

Date:_____

Notes:

_____

_____

_____

_____

_____

_____

_____

_____

_____

_____

_____

_____

_____

Could this have been an email? ☐ Yes ☐ No

Date:_____

Notes:

_____

_____

_____

_____

_____

_____

_____

_____

_____

_____

_____

_____

_____

Could this have been an email? ☐ Yes ☐ No

Date:_____

Notes:

_____

_____

_____

_____

_____

_____

_____

_____

_____

_____

_____

_____

Could this have been an email? ☐ Yes ☐ No

Date:_____

Notes:

_____

_____

_____

_____

_____

_____

_____

_____

_____

_____

_____

_____

_____

_____

Could this have been an email? ☐ Yes ☐ No

Date:_____

Notes:

_____

_____

_____

_____

_____

_____

_____

_____

_____

_____

_____

_____

_____

Could this have been an email? ☐ Yes ☐ No

Date:_____

Notes:

_____

_____

_____

_____

_____

_____

_____

_____

_____

_____

_____

_____

_____

Could this have been an email? ☐ Yes ☐ No

Date:_____

Notes:

_____

_____

_____

_____

_____

_____

_____

_____

_____

_____

_____

_____

_____

Could this have been an email? ☐ Yes ☐ No

Date:_____

Notes:

_____

_____

_____

_____

_____

_____

_____

_____

_____

_____

_____

_____

_____

_____

_____

Could this have been an email? ☐ Yes ☐ No

Date:_____

Notes:

_____

_____

_____

_____

_____

_____

_____

_____

_____

_____

_____

_____

_____

Could this have been an email? ☐ Yes ☐ No

Date:_____

Notes:

_____

_____

_____

_____

_____

_____

_____

_____

_____

_____

_____

_____

_____

_____

Could this have been an email? ☐ Yes ☐ No

Date:_____

Notes:

_____

_____

_____

_____

_____

_____

_____

_____

_____

_____

_____

_____

_____

Could this have been an email? ☐ Yes ☐ No

Date:_____

Notes:

_____

_____

_____

_____

_____

_____

_____

_____

_____

_____

_____

_____

_____

_____

_____

Could this have been an email? ☐ Yes ☐ No

Date:_____

Notes:

_____

_____

_____

_____

_____

_____

_____

_____

_____

_____

_____

_____

_____

_____

Could this have been an email? ☐ Yes ☐ No

Date:_____

Notes:

_____

_____

_____

_____

_____

_____

_____

_____

_____

_____

_____

_____

_____

_____

Could this have been an email? ☐ Yes ☐ No

Date:_____

Notes:

_____

_____

_____

_____

_____

_____

_____

_____

_____

_____

_____

_____

_____

Could this have been an email? ☐ Yes ☐ No

Date:_____

Notes:

_____

_____

_____

_____

_____

_____

_____

_____

_____

_____

_____

_____

_____

_____

Could this have been an email? ☐ Yes ☐ No

Date:_____

Notes:

_____

_____

_____

_____

_____

_____

_____

_____

_____

_____

_____

_____

_____

_____

_____

Could this have been an email? ☐ Yes ☐ No

Date:_____

Notes:

_____

_____

_____

_____

_____

_____

_____

_____

_____

_____

_____

_____

_____

_____

Could this have been an email? ☐ Yes ☐ No

Date:_____

Notes:

_____

_____

_____

_____

_____

_____

_____

_____

_____

_____

_____

_____

Could this have been an email? ☐ Yes ☐ No

Date:_____

Notes:

_____

_____

_____

_____

_____

_____

_____

_____

_____

_____

_____

_____

_____

_____

Could this have been an email? ☐ Yes ☐ No

Date:_____

Notes:

_____

_____

_____

_____

_____

_____

_____

_____

_____

_____

_____

_____

Could this have been an email? ☐ Yes ☐ No

Date:_____

Notes:

_____

_____

_____

_____

_____

_____

_____

_____

_____

_____

_____

_____

_____

Could this have been an email? ☐ Yes ☐ No

Date:_____

Notes:

_____

_____

_____

_____

_____

_____

_____

_____

_____

_____

_____

Could this have been an email? ☐ Yes ☐ No

Date:_____

Notes:

_____

_____

_____

_____

_____

_____

_____

_____

_____

_____

_____

_____

_____

_____

_____

Could this have been an email? ☐ Yes ☐ No

Date:_____

Notes:

_____

_____

_____

_____

_____

_____

_____

_____

_____

_____

_____

_____

Could this have been an email? ☐ Yes ☐ No

Date:_____

Notes:

_____

_____

_____

_____

_____

_____

_____

_____

_____

_____

_____

_____

_____

_____

Could this have been an email? ☐ Yes ☐ No

Date:_____

Notes:

_____

_____

_____

_____

_____

_____

_____

_____

_____

_____

_____

_____

Could this have been an email? ☐ Yes ☐ No

Date:_____

Notes:

_____

_____

_____

_____

_____

_____

_____

_____

_____

_____

_____

_____

_____

_____

Could this have been an email? ☐ Yes ☐ No

Date:_____

Notes:

_____

_____

_____

_____

_____

_____

_____

_____

_____

_____

_____

_____

_____

Could this have been an email? ☐ Yes ☐ No

Date:_____

Notes:

_____

_____

_____

_____

_____

_____

_____

_____

_____

_____

_____

_____

Could this have been an email? ☐ Yes ☐ No

Date:_____

Notes:

_____

_____

_____

_____

_____

_____

_____

_____

_____

_____

_____

_____

Could this have been an email? ☐ Yes ☐ No

Date:_____

Notes:

_____

_____

_____

_____

_____

_____

_____

_____

_____

_____

_____

_____

_____

_____

Could this have been an email? ☐ Yes ☐ No

Date:_____

Notes:

_____

_____

_____

_____

_____

_____

_____

_____

_____

_____

_____

_____

_____

Could this have been an email? ☐ Yes ☐ No

Date:_____

Notes:

_____

_____

_____

_____

_____

_____

_____

_____

_____

_____

_____

_____

_____

Could this have been an email? ☐ Yes ☐ No

Date:_____

Notes:

_____

_____

_____

_____

_____

_____

_____

_____

_____

_____

_____

Could this have been an email? ☐ Yes ☐ No

Date:_____

Notes:

_____

_____

_____

_____

_____

_____

_____

_____

_____

_____

_____

_____

_____

_____

Could this have been an email? ☐ Yes ☐ No

Date:_____

Notes:

_____

_____

_____

_____

_____

_____

_____

_____

_____

_____

_____

_____

_____

Could this have been an email? ☐ Yes ☐ No

Date:_____

Notes:

_____

_____

_____

_____

_____

_____

_____

_____

_____

_____

_____

_____

_____

_____

Could this have been an email? ☐ Yes ☐ No

Date:_____

Notes:

_____

_____

_____

_____

_____

_____

_____

_____

_____

_____

_____

_____

Could this have been an email? ☐ Yes ☐ No

Date:_____

Notes:

_____
_____
_____
_____
_____
_____
_____
_____
_____
_____
_____
_____
_____

Could this have been an email? ☐ Yes ☐ No

Date:_____

Notes:

_____

_____

_____

_____

_____

_____

_____

_____

_____

_____

_____

_____

_____

_____

Could this have been an email? ☐ Yes ☐ No

Date:_____

Notes:

_____

_____

_____

_____

_____

_____

_____

_____

_____

_____

_____

_____

_____

Could this have been an email? ☐ Yes ☐ No

Date:_____

Notes:

_____

_____

_____

_____

_____

_____

_____

_____

_____

_____

_____

_____

Could this have been an email? ☐ Yes ☐ No

Date:_____

Notes:

_____
_____
_____
_____
_____
_____
_____
_____
_____
_____
_____
_____
_____

Could this have been an email? ☐ Yes ☐ No

Date:_____

Notes:

_____

_____

_____

_____

_____

_____

_____

_____

_____

_____

_____

_____

_____

Could this have been an email? ☐ Yes ☐ No

Date:_____

Notes:

_____

_____

_____

_____

_____

_____

_____

_____

_____

_____

_____

_____

_____

Could this have been an email? ☐ Yes ☐ No

Date:_____

Notes:

_____

_____

_____

_____

_____

_____

_____

_____

_____

_____

_____

_____

_____

Could this have been an email? ☐ Yes ☐ No

Date:_____

Notes:

_____

_____

_____

_____

_____

_____

_____

_____

_____

_____

_____

_____

_____

Could this have been an email? ☐ Yes ☐ No

Date:_____

Notes:

_____

_____

_____

_____

_____

_____

_____

_____

_____

_____

_____

_____

_____

Could this have been an email? ☐ Yes ☐ No

Date:_____

Notes:

_____

_____

_____

_____

_____

_____

_____

_____

_____

_____

_____

_____

_____

_____

Could this have been an email? ☐ Yes ☐ No

Date:_____

Notes:

_____

_____

_____

_____

_____

_____

_____

_____

_____

_____

_____

_____

_____

Could this have been an email? ☐ Yes ☐ No

Date:_____

Notes:

_____

_____

_____

_____

_____

_____

_____

_____

_____

_____

_____

_____

_____

_____

Could this have been an email? ☐ Yes ☐ No

Date:_____

Notes:

_____

_____

_____

_____

_____

_____

_____

_____

_____

_____

_____

_____

_____

Could this have been an email? ☐ Yes ☐ No

Date:_____

Notes:

_____

_____

_____

_____

_____

_____

_____

_____

_____

_____

_____

_____

_____

Could this have been an email? ☐ Yes ☐ No

Date:_____

Notes:

_____

_____

_____

_____

_____

_____

_____

_____

_____

_____

_____

_____

Could this have been an email? ☐ Yes ☐ No

Date:_____

Notes:

_____

_____

_____

_____

_____

_____

_____

_____

_____

_____

_____

_____

_____

_____

Could this have been an email? ☐ Yes ☐ No

Date:_____

Notes:

_____

_____

_____

_____

_____

_____

_____

_____

_____

_____

_____

_____

Could this have been an email? ☐ Yes ☐ No

Date:_____

Notes:

_____

_____

_____

_____

_____

_____

_____

_____

_____

_____

_____

_____

_____

Could this have been an email? ☐ Yes ☐ No

Date:_____

Notes:

_____

_____

_____

_____

_____

_____

_____

_____

_____

_____

_____

_____

_____

Could this have been an email? ☐ Yes ☐ No

Date:_____

Notes:

_____

_____

_____

_____

_____

_____

_____

_____

_____

_____

_____

_____

_____

_____

Could this have been an email? ☐ Yes ☐ No

Date:_____

Notes:

_____

_____

_____

_____

_____

_____

_____

_____

_____

_____

_____

_____

_____

Could this have been an email? ☐ Yes ☐ No

Date:_____

Notes:

_____

_____

_____

_____

_____

_____

_____

_____

_____

_____

_____

_____

_____

Could this have been an email? ☐ Yes ☐ No

Date:_____

Notes:

_____

_____

_____

_____

_____

_____

_____

_____

_____

_____

_____

_____

_____

Could this have been an email? ☐ Yes ☐ No

Date:_____

Notes:

_____

_____

_____

_____

_____

_____

_____

_____

_____

_____

_____

_____

_____

_____

Could this have been an email? ☐ Yes ☐ No

Date:_____

Notes:

_____

_____

_____

_____

_____

_____

_____

_____

_____

_____

_____

_____

_____

Could this have been an email? ☐ Yes ☐ No

Date:_____

Notes:

_____

_____

_____

_____

_____

_____

_____

_____

_____

_____

_____

_____

_____

_____

_____

Could this have been an email? ☐ Yes ☐ No

Date:_____

Notes:

_____

_____

_____

_____

_____

_____

_____

_____

_____

_____

_____

_____

Could this have been an email? ☐ Yes ☐ No

Date:_____

Notes:

_____

_____

_____

_____

_____

_____

_____

_____

_____

_____

_____

_____

_____

Could this have been an email? ☐ Yes ☐ No

Date:_____

Notes:

_____
_____
_____
_____
_____
_____
_____
_____
_____
_____
_____
_____
_____

Could this have been an email? ☐ Yes ☐ No

Date:_____

Notes:

_____

_____

_____

_____

_____

_____

_____

_____

_____

_____

_____

_____

_____

Could this have been an email? ☐ Yes ☐ No

Date:_____

Notes:

_____

_____

_____

_____

_____

_____

_____

_____

_____

_____

_____

_____

Could this have been an email? ☐ Yes ☐ No

Made in the USA
Las Vegas, NV
07 December 2022

61408636R00057